Contents

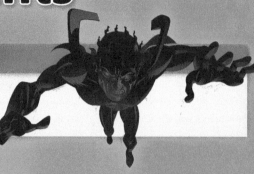

Written by
Diana Bentley
Sylvia Karavis
Illustrated by
Peter Richardson

Series editor **Dee Reid**

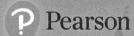

Pearson

Characters

Agent Em

Agent Vee

Agent Que

Agent Zed

Scorcher

Tricky words

- suddenly
- crackled
- appeared
- destroy
- starve
- weakness
- scorched
- cannon

Read these words to the student. Help them with these words when they appear in the text.

Introduction

The four agents were in their Base when suddenly all the alarms went off and an evil face appeared on their screen. It is Scorcher, the super-villain, who plans to destroy all the crops and watch as humans starve. He tells the agents that he will burn them alive if they try to stop him. Em thinks she has found his weakness but will her plan work?

SCORCHER

The agents were in the Base when suddenly the alarms went off.

Then the blank screen crackled into life and an evil face appeared.

"I am Scorcher.
I will destroy all the crops in the world with my fire.
I will watch as all humans starve.
Don't try to stop me or I will burn you alive."

Then the screen went blank.

The agents looked at each other.
"We have to stop Scorcher," said Em.
"Or all the humans in the world will die," said Zed.
"We can try, but we might be turned into toast," said Que.

Suddenly a ball of fire hit the Base
and flames burned all around.
The agents heard Scorcher laughing.

"You can't stop me! I will burn your crops and watch the world starve."

SCORCHER

"What can we do?" asked Que.
"We must face him," said Em.
"Are you mad?" said Vee. "He will
burn us and the crops."
"I just might have found his weakness," said Em
and she told the other agents her plan.

The agents went outside.
The crops were burning all around them.

"Stop!" yelled Em at Scorcher.
Scorcher turned around.
"I told you what I would do to you," he yelled and he shot a ball of fire at Em.

Em's clothes burst into flames.
The flames scorched her hands and face.

Suddenly a jet of water hit Em
and the flames died away.
The other agents had turned
a water cannon on her.

Then they turned the water cannon on Scorcher.

A jet of water hit Scorcher.
The water hit his hands and the flames died away.
But when the water hit his face, it burned his skin.

"Aaaah!" he screamed.

"You have stopped me now, but I will be back!" said Scorcher. Then he flew away.

"Are you OK?" asked Zed.

"Not quite toast!" laughed Em.

"How did you know water would burn his face?" asked Vee.

"From the computer, you idiots!" said Em.

The others laughed.

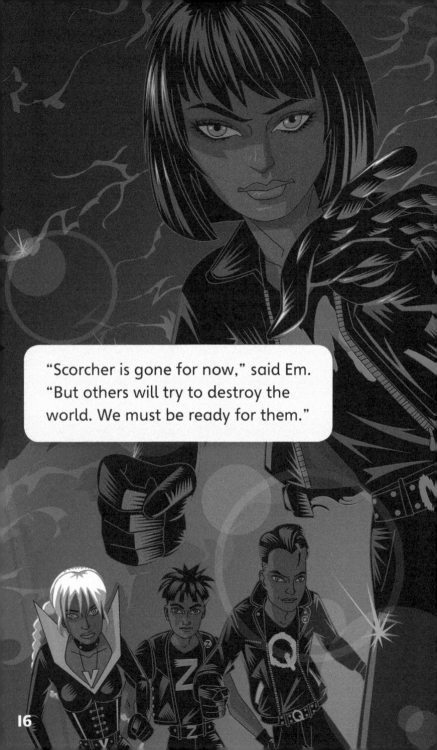

"Scorcher is gone for now," said Em. "But others will try to destroy the world. We must be ready for them."

Quiz ////////////////////////

Text comprehension

Literal comprehension
p4 What was Scorcher's evil plan?
p12 What was Em's plan to get rid of Scorcher?

Inferential comprehension
p4 How can you tell Scorcher is evil?
p5 Why does Que think the agents might be turned into toast?
p7 What does Vee think of Em's plan?

Personal response
• Do you think Em is brave?
• Would you face Scorcher?

Word knowledge

p4 Find two adjectives.
p7 How many sentences are on this page?
p10 Find a word meaning 'shouted'.

Spelling challenge

Read these words:
asked   know   when
Now try to spell them!

Ha! Ha! Ha!

What's big, green and never smiles?

The Incredible Sulk!

Find out about

- a bush fire in Australia which killed
  173 people and thousands of animals.

Tricky words

- terrible
- roaring
- neighbour
- radiator
- thousands
- koala
- usually
- survivors

Read these words to the student. Help them with these words when they appear in the text.

Introduction

In Australia in 2009 there were terrible bush fires. People knew what to do. They had had bush fires before, but these fires were worse. The fires spread quickly because there were strong winds. People tried to escape but roads were blocked by burning trees. Many people were trapped.

The Worst Fire

People heard the fire warning on the radio. They knew what to do. They had had bush fires before. They got their hoses ready in case the fire got too close.

That night they went to bed.
But no-one knew what terrible
danger they were in.

In the night 400 fires broke out.
The fires spread quickly because
there were strong winds.

People woke to the terrible sound
of roaring flames.
They tried to escape but the roads
were blocked by burning trees
and fallen power lines.

Many people were trapped.
Some people ran into a wall of
flames as they tried to escape.

The people in one town thought the fire was too far off to get them. Then the wind changed and the flames raced towards them. Burning trees blocked the roads and 50 people were trapped by the roaring flames. Some of them died in the fire.

One man saw his neighbour on fire.
The only water he had was in his car radiator.
He threw the water over the burning man.
One man put his children into the car then he
went back into the house to get something.
When he went back out his car was on fire.

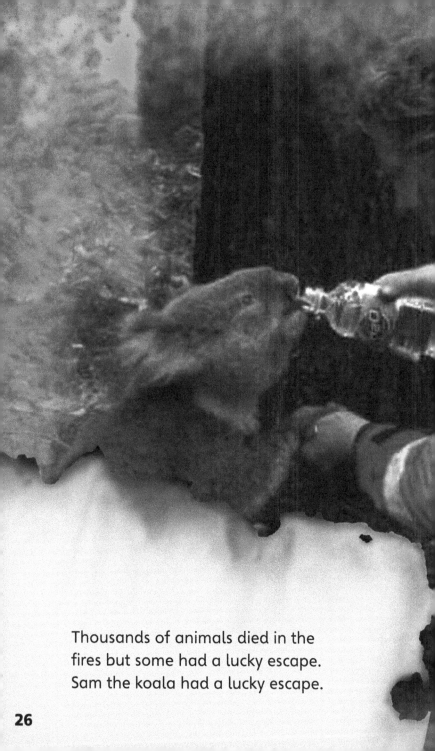

Thousands of animals died in the
fires but some had a lucky escape.
Sam the koala had a lucky escape.

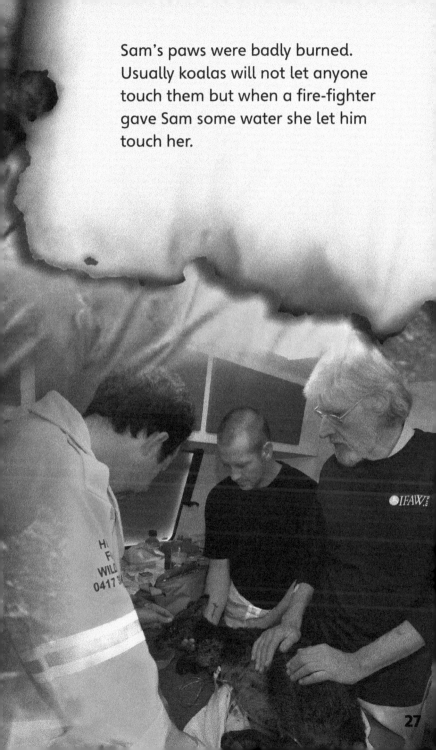

Sam's paws were badly burned. Usually koalas will not let anyone touch them but when a fire-fighter gave Sam some water she let him touch her.

He took Sam to the animal shelter.
There was another koala in the shelter.
The fire-fighters called him Bob.

Bob and Sam clung to each other.
But Sam was too badly burned and she died.

Survivors told of the bravery of their friends and neighbours and the fire-fighters who went back into the fires to try to save people.

When the fires stopped, 173 people had died in the flames and over 2000 houses were burned to the ground.

Quiz ////////////////////

Spelling challenge

Read these words:

took   always   night

Now try to spell them!

Ha! Ha! Ha!

What is an Australian's favourite drink?

Coca-koala!